Roe HenryMorse JohnSouthworth JohnPlessington PhilipEvans John

eKirby RichardGwyn MargaretClitherow MargaretWard EdwardGe

MAGNIFICENT WITNESSES

ughton RobertLawrence AugustineWebster RobertReynolds JohnSto

MAGNIFICENT WITNESSES

40 English and Welsh Martyrs

by Martin P. Harney, S.J.

St. Paul Editions

Permissu Superiorum S.J.

NIHIL OBSTAT:
    John G. Hogan
        Diocesan Censor

IMPRIMATUR:
  Richard Cardinal Cushing
    ✛ *Archbishop of Boston*

August 13, 1970

Library of Congress Catalog Card Number: *71 – 142749*

COPYRIGHT, 1970, BY THE DAUGHTERS OF ST. PAUL
PRINTED IN THE U.S.A. BY THE DAUGHTERS OF ST. PAUL
50 ST. PAUL'S AVENUE, JAMAICA PLAIN
BOSTON, MA. 02130

TO

HIS EMINENCE RICHARD CARDINAL CUSHING, D.D.

WITH SINCEREST GRATITUDE FOR

HIS HOLY PASTORAL CARE AND HIS INDOMITABLY

BRAVE EXAMPLE.

ACKNOWLEDGMENTS

Grateful acknowledgment is made to P.J. Kenedy and Sons, a subsidiary of Crowell, Collier and Macmillan, of New York, for permission to quote from *Butler's Lives of the Saints*, "Complete Edition, Edited, Revised and Supplemented by Herbert Thurston, S.J. and Donald Attwater." Four Volumes, New York, 1956. Vol. I. p. 436, reply of Bd. Anne Line; p. 682, thanksgiving of Bd. Margaret Clitherow. Vol. III, p. 384, incident of Bd. John Kemble's pipe; p. 587, denial of charges by Bd. Ambrose Barlow, O.S.B.; Vol. IV. p. 203, replies of Bd. Richard Gwyn and of his wife; p. 448, Statement of Bd. Cuthbert Mayne on Queen's religious supremacy; p. 468, statement of Bd. Edmund Campion, S.J.; p. 535, statement of Bd. John Roberts, O.S.B.

Grateful acknowledgment is also due to *The Wanderer*, "A National Catholic Weekly," and to its associate-editor, Alphonse J. Matt, Jr., for permission to quote from the article of Rev. Francis J. Ripley, "The English Martyrs," which appeared in the edition of June 18, 1970. The quotations are all on page 6. They are (1) incidents and remarks of Bd. Robert Southwell, S.J., Bd. Philip Howard, Earl of Arundel, Bd. Henry Morse, S.J., Bd. John Lloyd, Bd. John Kemble, Bd. David Lewis, S.J.; and (2) two summaries of persecutory legislation.

A very special thanks is owing to Father Clement Tigar, S.J., Vice-Postulator of the Cause of the English and the Welsh Martyrs for his identification of Bd. John Stone, O.S.A., and for his kindly encouragement.

MARTIN P. HARNEY, S.J.

11

Faith of Our Fathers

Faith of our fathers, living still
    In spite of dungeon, fire and sword;
Oh, how our hearts beat high with joy
    Whene'er we hear that glorious word!
Faith of our fathers! Holy Faith!
    We will be true to thee till death.
    (Repeat)

Our fathers, chained in prisons dark,
    Were still in heart and conscience free;
How sweet would be their children's fate,
    If they, like them, could die for thee!
Faith of our fathers! Holy Faith!
    We will be true to thee till death.
    (Repeat)

Faith of our fathers, we will love
    Both friend and foe in all our strife,
And preach thee too, as love knows how
    By kindly words and virtuous life:
Faith of our fathers! Holy Faith!
    We will be true to thee till death.
    (Repeat)

FATHER F. W. FABER

Foreword

Who were these forty martyrs? They were religious, priests and layfolk, who during the years 1535 to 1681 freely suffered death for the Catholic Faith, and particularly for its doctrine of the universal spiritual jurisdiction of the Holy See of Rome. They were martyrs for the Primacy of the Popes. On May 18, 1970, in announcing their coming canonization, Pope Paul VI summarized the glory of the forty martyrs: "In a special way these Martyrs gave outstanding evidence of a sincere Faith which is entirely foreign to false contortions in very holy matters. By this sincere Faith one manifests his personal persuasion without fear. It is this which is a necessary condition of every true and fruitful ecumenical dialogue. These Martyrs particularly show the example of true Christian charity towards those also who do not profess the same Christian Faith. Not without being moved does one note that, in an age when religious controversy so greatly stirred up hatred, this was plainly absent from these

13

heroes of the Christian Faith. These Blessed Martyrs give an outstanding witness to human dignity and liberty. We trust that they may contribute to the promotion of true ecumenism and the efficacious protection of true values on which rests the real peace and prosperity of human society." On October 25, 1970, Pope Paul VI canonized these forty martyrs.

The passions of the forty martyrs are not being recounted here to stir up old bitternesses, but to inspire all with the narrative of their heroic constancies; they were undyingly loyal to their Catholic Religion and its fundamental doctrine of the papal primacy.

MARTIN P. HARNEY, S.J.

14

CONTENTS

CONTENTS

16

The	Martyrs
Forty	under
Martyrs	Henry VIII

The act of Royal Supremacy, passed in November 1534, provided that the king of England should be acknowledged as the only supreme head on earth of the Church in England. This supremacy was made to extend to faith, worship and discipline; in the future even bishops were to receive the spiritualities of their sees from the king alone. In the following year there followed a formal renunciation of the Pope. The denial of Royal Supremacy was declared an act of high treason, and was to be punished as such by hanging,

17

drawing and quartering.[1] In the bloody enforcement that followed, the most illustrious victims were St. John Fisher, the holy and courageous bishop of Rochester, and St. Thomas More, the brilliant humanist and learned lawyer. Both had maintained openly that the Papal Supremacy was the only true doctrine and that the Royal Supremacy had never been held in England. Both were beheaded. Both were canonized in 1935.

1. The condemned was bound, placed prone on a low sled, which was dragged by horses over the rough roads to the place of execution. He was then hanged from a gallows. While still alive he was cut down and disemboweled; when he was dead his corpse was quartered. Long before Henry VIII's time this was the punishment for treason.

1. St. John Houghton
2. St. Robert Lawrence
3. St. Augustine Webster
   Carthusians, and
4. St. Robert Reynolds,
   Brigittine monk

All were executed at Tyburn,
   May 4, 1535

On or about April 13, 1535, John
Houghton, prior of the London Charter-
house, was committed to the Tower. He
was soon joined by Robert Lawrence,
prior of Beauvale, Nottinghamshire,
Augustine Webster, prior of Axholme,
Lincolnshire, and Richard Reynolds, a
Brigittine monk of Syon Abbey. All were
saintly religious; Richard Reynolds was
renowned for his learning. All had refused
to take the oath of supremacy. They were
tried and condemned as traitors because
they had denied that Henry VIII was head
of the Church in England. At the last
moment pardons were offered them if
they would acknowledge Henry's suprem-

acy. They refused. All were hanged in their habits, an added indignity. St. John died first, after embracing his executioner and publicly proclaiming that he was being done to death because he would not deny a doctrine of the Church. He was conscious all through the cruel mutilations. The rest of the martyrs displayed the same courage. An effort was made to break the spirit of St. Richard; because he was last, he was forced to witness the terrible barbarities inflicted on his companions. He did not fail. The date of their witness was May 4, 1535.

5. St. John Stone, O.S.A.
Canterbury,
1539

Three things are known for certain about St. John. He was an Austin friar, he was a Doctor of Divinity, learned and prayerful, and he was martyred at the Dane-John, Canterbury. Very probably he was the Austin friar of whose "insolence" Ingworth, one of the King's visitors, complained to Cromwell: "at all times he still held, and still desired to die for it, that the King may not be head of the Church of England." He seems to have been held in prison for a long time, during which he added voluntary mortifications to his enforced sufferings. The expense account, filed by the City Chancellor of Canterbury, for the execution of "ffryer Stone" contains the item, "for a Halter to hang hym....1 d."

The Forty Martyrs

Martyrs under Queen Elizabeth I

The forty-four years of Elizabeth's reign were for Catholics a period of incessant persecution. It must suffice only to instance the laws which made the profession and the practice of Catholicism high treason, punishable with frightful death penalties. The new Act of Supremacy made it high treason to maintain the Pope's authority; it also imposed an oath acknowledging the queen as "Supreme Governess in matters spiritual." A new Act of Uniformity restored *The Book of Common Prayer*, prohibited the Mass and made attendance at Protestant churches compulsory. After Elizabeth's excommunication new laws made it treason to call the queen a heretic, to introduce papal bulls, to absolve or reconcile with the Catholic Church any person, or to be absolved or reconciled. Even to harbor a priest brought on the death penalty. A law of 1585 provided that any Jesuit or Seminary Priest remaining in England over forty days, or any English subject studying at a foreign seminary, and not returning within sixty days to take the oath of royal supremacy, should suffer the penalties of high treason. In consequence all priests had to lead furtive existences, moving about stealthily and in disguise, and hiding in remote country-houses or in secret city-dwellings. To discover these hidden priests the whole land swarmed with spies and priest-hunters (pursuivants).

6. St. Cuthbert Mayne
Seminary Priest
Launceston, Cornwall
November 29, 1577

St. Cuthbert was the first martyr of the Seminary Priests.[1] He was a converted minister of the Established Church. He had strong internal Catholic convictions, and these were strengthened by letters from former Oxford friends, now refugees at Douay, Dr. Gregory Martin and St. Edmund Campion. One such letter, falling into the hands of the Bishop of London, brought the pursuivants to Oxford seeking him. He escaped and embarked for Flanders. He became a Catholic in 1573 at the Douay Seminary, was ordained in 1575, and set out for England the following year. He took up his residence with a staunch Catholic, Sir Francis Tregian, appearing as his land-steward.

1. Since there were no longer any Catholic dioceses, the secular priests labored wherever they could throughout England. As their studies were made at the English Seminaries of Douay, Rome and Valladolid, they were called "the Seminary Priests."

He was arrested a year later by the High-Sheriff, Sir Richard Grenville. He was confined in a filthy prison until his trial. It was a farcical performance; on the poorest of evidence he was condemned as a traitor. The day before his execution the martyr was offered his freedom if he would swear to the Queen's ecclesiastical supremacy. St. Cuthbert asked for a Bible, made the Sign of the Cross, and kissed the sacred volume; and then his words came clear and firm: "The Queen never was, nor is, nor ever shall be, the head of the Church of England." On November 29, 1577, St. Cuthbert Mayne was hanged in the market-place of Launceston. He was cut down, but probably died in the butcheries.

7. St. Edmund Campion, S.J.
Tyburn
December 1, 1581

St. Edmund Campion is the most widely known of the Forty Martyrs; so many writers have honored his intelligence, eloquence, energy and heroism. He had just attained manhood when he was accounted the most brilliant scholar at Oxford. Yet he was very unhappy. He had taken the oath of supremacy. But his readings of the Fathers of the Church and his own Catholic tendencies were shaking his allegiance to Anglicanism. He left Oxford for Dublin, where his papist views grew stronger. Eventually he fled to the Douay Seminary in 1571. After two years he went to Rome and joined the Society of Jesus.

Cardinal Allen, the leader of the English exiles, persuaded Pope Gregory XIII to send some English Jesuits to their home country. Father Robert Persons and Father Edmund Campion were chosen, and left Rome in 1580. They carried a sworn statement that their purpose was purely religious and that they were forbidden to mix in politics. Disguised, they succeeded in entering England. But the government had been forewarned; and so close was the search for them that they had to separate. St. Edmund labored first in the Midlands. Proceeding with utmost caution he rode on horseback through the countrysides. He reaped a rich harvest, strengthening the Catholics and gaining back influential persons. Later he went to Lancashire, where he preached almost daily and with marvelous success; even fifty years later Lancashire folk spoke of his moving eloquence. Of course his hairbreadth escapes continued.

All this time he was writing a pamphlet, *Decem Rationes*, in which he explained the ten reasons why he challenged the most learned Anglican divines to discuss religion with him. The printing had to be done with the greatest secrecy. The little work proved a tremendous sensation, especially when four hundred copies were found on the benches of the

University Church, Oxford. The attention of the whole country was now drawn to Campion. Efforts to capture him were redoubled. He was taken three weeks later in Norfolk.

Indignities were heaped upon St. Edmund as he was brought to the Tower of London. After three days in the "Little Ease," a cell so narrow that a prisoner could neither walk, stand, lie nor sit, he was interviewed by three high officials (one, it is said, was the Queen). Bribes of liberty and preferment were offered, and refused. They would be offered again, after the condemnation; and again they would be refused. Later he was racked. While still suffering from that painful torture, Campion was given his asked-for discussion; four times he was confronted by Anglican dignitaries. Despite his agonies he acquitted himself effectively. Again he was racked. On November 14, together with St. Ralph Sherwin, Blessed Thomas Cottam, St. Luke Kirby and others, St. Edmund Campion was tried and condemned. He was too weak to raise his tortured arm; one of his companions, kissing his hand, raised it up for him.

Before the sentencing St. Edmund addressed the Court: "In condemning us you condemn all your ancestors.... To be condemned with these old lights — not of England only, but of the world — by their degenerate descendants, is both gladness and glory to us. God lives, posterity will live. Their judgment is not so liable to corruption as that of those who sentence us to death."

On December 1, St. Edmund Campion, S.J. with St. Ralph Sherwin and St. Alexander Briant, S.J. were drawn to Tyburn and hanged there. St. Edmund stood at the gallows, cheerful, pleasant, and courageous.

8. St. Ralph Sherwin
Seminary Priest
Tyburn
December 1, 1581

St. Ralph Sherwin was the first martyr of the English College of Rome. He had had a distinguished career at Oxford. In 1575 he was converted at Douay, and he was ordained there in 1577. He went to the English College of Rome for further studies. He was in the party that in 1580 set out for England. After six months' ministry he was arrested and put in chains at the Marshalsea prison; later he was transferred to the Tower. He was racked cruelly twice. A bishopric was offered to him if he would apostatize. After a year in prison St. Ralph was condemned along with St. Edmund Campion. Bravely and truly he declared: "The plain reason of our standing here is religion and not treason." He ascended the scaffold right after St. Edmund. St. Ralph Sherwin was thirty-one years of age when he made the supreme sacrifice.

9. St. Alexander Briant, S.J.
Tyburn
December 1, 1581

St. Alexander Briant, S.J. was laid on the same sled with St. Ralph Sherwin going to Tyburn. St. Alexander, after being secretly reconciled at Oxford, went to Rheims where he was ordained. He came back to England in 1578 and labored in Somersetshire. He was captured, April 28, 1581, and was imprisoned in the Tower, where he was subjected to excruciating tortures. To the rack, starvation and cold was added the inhuman forcing of needles under his nails. It was during this confinement that St. Alexander requested and was given admission into the Society of Jesus. He made his novitiate in prison. Condemned with St. Edmund Campion and St. Ralph Sherwin, he was executed with them on December 1, 1581. Through the malice or carelessness of the executioner he was put to needless sufferings. He was in his twenty-seventh year.

31

10. St. John Payne
Seminary Priest
Chelmsford
April 2, 1582

St. John Payne first appears as a seminarian at Douay in 1574. There he was ordained a priest in 1576. In that year with St. Cuthbert Mayne he returned to England. He labored zealously in Essex. He was once arrested and imprisoned there. The last time that he was seized he was in Warwickshire; it was in July, 1581. He was brought to London Tower, where he was racked on two occasions. St. John was tried in Chelmsford for a plot against the Queen's life. It was completely fictitious. The sole witness was an evil-living Catholic, one Eliot, notorious as a profligate, embezzler and murderer. He was known as "Judas" Eliot, because he had denounced more than thirty priests and had caused the capture of St. Edmund Campion. On this scoundrel's uncorroborated testimony St. John was condemned. The spectators prevented the barbarities until he was dead. St. John Payne was martyred on April 2, 1582.

11. St. Luke Kirby
Seminary Priest
Tyburn
May 30, 1582

St. Luke Kirby was converted and studied at Douay in 1576, was ordained in 1577, and finished his studies in Rome. Immediately on landing at Dover, in June 1580, he was arrested. He was eventually brought to London Tower. There on December 9, he was tortured for more than an hour in the terrible "Scavenger's Daughter." This was a broad iron hoop in which the body, hands, feet, and head of the victim were forced into one ball. Such was the excess of its compression that the blood was started from the nose and the extremities of the hands and feet. St. Luke was condemned on November 17. He rejected the sheriff's pardon if he would forsake the Man of Rome, declaring that to deny the Pope's authority was to deny a doctrine of faith, an action which would damn his soul. St. Luke Kirby was martyred on May 30, 1582.

12. St. Richard Gwyn
Layman
Wrexham
October 15, 1584

St. Richard Gwyn, the protomartyr of Wales, was born about 1537. He was a schoolmaster in North Wales. He and his wife, Catherine, had six children. For a time he had conformed in religion; but he was reconciled when missionary priests came to Wales. Owing to his recusancy he was arrested more than once. From 1579, when he spurned the bribe of his liberty, he was kept in prison until his death. He was frequently treated most opprobriously. Once he was put in the stocks all day and was heckled continuously by heretical ministers. One of them loudly protested that he had the power of the keys as much as St. Peter; but he also had a conspicuously red nose. Poor Richard, exasperated, retorted, "There is this difference: whereas St. Peter received the keys of the Kingdom of Heaven, you appear to have received those of the beer-cellar!" At one time St. Richard was heavily fined for his recusancy, 2,480 pounds (modern money). The judge asked him what means he had to pay this enormous fine. He answered, "I have somewhat towards it."

"How much?"

"Six pence," was his reply.

St. Richard was tried and convicted of treason at Wrexham in October, 1584. Three chief witnesses were bribed to give false evidence. The jury refused to convict. Another jury was impanelled; they inquired of the judge whom they were to convict and whom they were to acquit. Mrs. Gwyn, with her babe in arms, was present; she was cautioned not to imitate her husband. Truly a heroine she spoke up to the sheriff, "If you lack blood, you may take my life as well as my husband's. If you will give the witnesses a little bribe, they will give evidence against me too." Again Richard was offered his life if he would acknowledge the Queen as the supreme head of the Church.

At St. Richard's execution, his wife, carrying their month-old son, knelt with her other children for his blessing. His last words were: "Jesus have mercy on me," spoken in his own Welsh language.

13. St. Margaret Clitherow
Laywoman
York
March 25, 1586

St. Margaret Clitherow, "the pearl of York," was born about 1556. She was brought up a Protestant, but was converted in 1571, three years after her marriage. Her husband, who remained a Protestant, was always devoted to her. Margaret was a charming person, possessed of good looks, witty and merry. She was a good housekeeper and a capable business woman. She was a deeply prayerful and disciplined soul. Above all Margaret was a fervent Catholic, continually risking her life hiding priests and preparing for the secret celebrations of Mass. Once she was imprisoned for two years in a loathsome cell of York Castle for her recusancy and suspected protection of priests.

Margaret Clitherow's final arrest came on March 14, 1586. She was arraigned in the York Assizes for harboring priests and hearing Mass. She refused to plead. She did this to protect her children and her friends, who would be the only witnesses, from being responsible for her death. The penalty in English law for refusing to plead was pressing to death. Margaret heard the terrible sentence serenely, saying: "God be thanked; all that He will send me is welcome. I am not worthy of so good a death as this." The day of her execution was set for March 25, 1586.

Part of the night before, St. Margaret endured an agony of fear. But she became calm, sewed her own shroud and spent the rest of the night on her knees. The next day, calmly, joyously, and smilingly, she walked barefooted to the place of execution. She was laid on the ground, a sharp stone was put beneath her spine, her arms were stretched in the form of a cross and bound to two posts. Then a door was placed upon her, and on it were piled stones to eight hundred weight. She was about a quarter of an hour in her agony. Her last words were: "Jesu, Jesu, Jesu, have mercy on me."

14. St. Margaret Ward
Laywoman
Tyburn
August 30, 1588

St. Margaret Ward, together with Blessed John Roche, her Irish servant, was arrested for accomplishing the escape of a priest, William Watson, from Bridewell prison in 1588. In vain both were tortured to reveal the whereabouts of the priest. Of St. Margaret's suffering St. Robert Southwell wrote: "She was flogged and hung up by the wrists, the tips of her toes only touching the ground for so long a time that she was crippled and paralyzed, but these sufferings greatly strengthened the glorious martyr for her last struggle." St. Margaret and Blessed John were condemned at Newgate prison. They were offered their liberty if they would attend Protestant worship. They refused. Together with four other martyrs they were executed on August 30, 1588. St. Margaret and her companions cheerfully sang hymns on their way to Tyburn's gallows.

15. St. Edward Gennings
    Seminary Priest
16. St. Swithin Wells
    Layman
17. St. Polydore Plasden
    Seminary Priest
18. St. Eustace White
    Seminary Priest
    The first two, Gray's Inn Fields;
    the second two, Tyburn
    All on December 10, 1591

Due to a royal proclamation in 1591 the laws against Catholics were sharply intensified. These four martyrs were the first victims. The three priests were condemned for their priesthood, the laymen for his harboring of a priest. St. Edmund Gennings, a native of Lichfield, was converted at the age of sixteen, and ordained a priest at Rheims in 1590. His apostolate was very brief; on November 7, 1591, he was arrested while saying Mass in London, at the home of St. Swithin Wells in Gray's Inn Fields. After his condemnation he was executed with horrible torturings near the site of his capture.

St. Swithin Wells until middle life had led a pleasant existence of a Hampshire country-gentleman. For many years he had conformed to the Established Religion. In 1583 he was reconciled to Catholicism. In 1585, he took up his residence at Gray's Inn Lane, London. He and his wife made their home a refuge-place for priests. St. Swithin was absent when St. Edmund Gennings was taken saying Mass. When he returned he was arrested and joined to the other captives, including his wife. All were condemned to death. St. Swithin was hanged right next to his home. Like St. Thomas More he joked on his way to death. His last words were to his executioner: "God pardon you and make you, Saul, a Paul.... I heartily forgive you."

St. Polydore Plasden, a Londoner, was but three years on the English mission. He was arrested with St. Edmund Gennings. Before his death at Tyburn he averred that he would forfeit a thousand lives rather than deny or fight against his faith. Sir Walter Raleigh ordered that he be not cut down until death had come.

St. Eustace White was the son of heretical parents. At his conversion he had to bear the sorrow of his father's curse. St. Eustace was ordained at Rome in 1586. The west of England was the scene of most of his mission. Apprehended September 1, 1591, he was sent to London and cast into the Bridewell. For forty-six days he was kept lying on straw with his hands closely chained. On October 25 orders came for his torturing. Seven times he was kept hanging by his manacled hands for hours at a time. He also suffered deprivation of food and clothing. He was condemned with St. Edmund, St. Polydore, and St. Swithin. On the scaffold at Tyburn he forgave Topcliffe [1] his cruelties. He declared to the people that his only treason was his priesthood.

1. Topcliffe, the priest-hunter, was the most infamous of the torturers. He was allowed to take his victims under warrant of the Privy Council to his own house in order to superintend their sufferings.

On being cut down he rose to his feet, only to be tripped and dragged to the place of butcheries, where he was held down by two powerful brutes until his terrible agonies were over.

19. St. John Boste
Seminary Priest
Durham
July 24, 1594

St. John Boste, born in Westmoreland, came of a good Northern Catholic family. He must have conformed at Oxford, but he was received into the Church in 1576. He was ordained in Rheims in 1581. Immediately he was sent to his own North Country. For twelve years he labored with such missionary zeal that the most extraordinary efforts were made to capture him. He was finally betrayed near Durham in 1593. Conveyed to London, St. John showed himself bold, joyful and pleasant despite his terrible racking—he was crippled permanently. Sent back to Durham in 1594 for his trial, St. John again behaved with undaunted courage and resolution. He induced a fellow-martyr, Blessed George Swalwell, a converted minister, who recanted through fear, to repent his cowardice, absolving him publicly in court. St. John recited the Angelus while mounting the ladder. Cut down while he was still very much alive, he was standing on his feet, and in that posture was cruelly butchered. His last words were a prayer for his executioner: "Jesus, Jesus, Jesus, forgive him!"

20. St. Robert Southwell, S.J. Tyburn February 21, 1595

For one man to have been a distinguished poet, a scion of nobility, a fervent religious, a tireless missioner and an heroic martyr is astonishing indeed. St. Robert Southwell was just such a man. Here only his missions and martyrdom can be treated. He became a Jesuit in 1578, was ordained in 1584, and was sent to England in 1586. He spent some six years in zealous and dangerous labors, either hidden in London or passing in various disguises from one house to another of the Catholic gentry. While he sojourned in London he became acquainted with St. Philip Howard, the Earl of Arundel, a prisoner for the faith. St. Robert was singularly gentle, and took no part in political intrigues or in the domestic disputes of the Catholics.

In 1592 St. Robert was arrested at Uxenden Hall, Harrow, through the

47

treachery of an unfortunate Catholic girl, a daughter of the house. Topcliffe, who effected the capture, wrote exultingly to the Queen: "I never did take so mighty a man, if he be rightly used." Twelve times he was tortured. Ten of these were in Topcliffe's own house, where the gentle, sensitive poet was hung from a wall by his hands with a sharp circle of iron around each wrist pressing on the artery, his legs bent backwards, his heels tied to his thighs. He was left hanging for seven hours at one stretch. But all that could be gotten out of him was: "My God and my all." Then for nearly three years he was confined in a verminous dungeon of the Tower. Finally he was tried and condemned for his priesthood. He was hanged at Tyburn, February 21, 1595. St. Robert, poet and martyr, had prayed for the crown of martyrdom; in his gentleness and human frailty he had dreaded it; in his holy courage he had embraced it.

21. St. Henry Walpole, S.J.
York
April 7, 1595

St. Henry Walpole, S.J. was yet a Protestant young man when at Tyburn he watched the execution of St. Edmund Campion. But the blood of the martyr stained his white doublet, and he sought admission into the Catholic religion. Shortly he was accepted by the Jesuit Order; and finally he was to receive the glory of martyrdom. In 1584 he was admitted into the Society of Jesus, and in 1588 he was ordained a priest. After acting as a chaplain to the Spanish forces in the Netherlands, he was at last sent on the English mission in 1590. He was arrested on December 7, two days after his landing on the northeast coast, and was imprisoned at York. He freely admitted that he was a Jesuit. The following February he was sent to the Tower of London, where he was frequently and severely racked. In the spring of 1595 he was sent back to York for trial. With

49

him was executed a Seminary priest, Blessed Alexander Rawlins. St. Henry was put to death last, and was forced to witness the horrible sufferings of his friend. He endured his cruel trials with the heroism of Blessed Alexander.

22. St. Philip Howard
Earl of Arundel
Prisoner, Tower of London
October 19, 1595

Philip Howard, Earl of Arundel, one of the highest nobles in Elizabethan England, was present at the disputation of St. Edmund Campion in the Tower. His impressions proved the first step in his conversion. But like most of Elizabeth's courtiers he was morally lax — he had even deserted his wife. He had many enemies, and after his wife's conversion to the Faith, he himself was suspected. She was one of the chief sustainers of Catholicism and of Catholic priests. The earl was now reconciled with her; indeed from then on he was intensely devoted to her. On September 30, 1584 Philip Howard was received into the Church and became a most fervent Catholic. The changes in his life were noted by his enemies, including the Queen, so that he resolved to flee, but not before writing a long and excellent letter of explanation to Elizabeth. The earl was captured at sea.

When he was returned, he was incarcerated in the Tower, where he remained a prisoner for ten years, until his death. Later, during the bloody persecutions following the Armada, he was tried for treason. The case was a farce, the evidence was patently fraudulent, as the Attorney General Popham admitted. St. Philip was left in prison. His last prayer, to see his wife and only son, who had been born after the start of his imprisonment, was refused except on condition of his coming to the Protestant church, on which terms he might also go free. His life in prison he made holy by his constant prayer and his practices of penance. St. Philip summed up his years of confinement in the inscription which he himself carved over the fireplace in Beauchamp Tower: "The more suffering for Christ in this life, the more glory with Christ in the life to come." St. Philip Howard, Earl of Arundel, died on October 19, 1595, in his thirty-eighth year. The wife he loved survived him until 1630.

23. St. John Jones, O.F.M.
Southwark
July 12, 1598

St. John was born in Caernarvonshire, of a Welsh family which had remained faithfully Catholic. In his early youth he joined the Franciscans. When the English Franciscan houses were finally dissolved, he found refuge in the French houses. After many years he went to Rome to beg that he might return to England. In 1592 the Franciscan superiors granted his request. For four years he labored in different parts of the country.

In 1596 St. John was betrayed to Topcliffe, who ordered his arrest. After cruel scourging the infamous priest-hunter took him to his own house and inflicted unspeakable tortures on him. The holy friar endured them with surprising fortitude. For two years more he was kept in prison. On July 3, 1598 St. John was convicted of high treason for having been ordained abroad and returning as a priest to England. From the gallows, set up in Southwark, he declared that he was dying for his faith, and that he was innocent of any political offense. The large crowd clearly showed their belief in him. But he was executed with the usual barbarities. St. John Jones, O.F.M. was martyred on July 12, 1598.

24. St. John Rigby
Layman
Southwark
June 21, 1600

St. John Rigby was one of the younger sons of a Lancashire gentleman. Due to family misfortunes he was obliged to enter domestic service. He worked for a Protestant family and was expected to attend the Established Church. He yielded and outwardly conformed. However, he was reconciled to the Church by St. John Jones, O.F.M., while the latter was in prison. A few years later, while defending another from the charge of recusancy, he was asked about his own convictions. John Rigby signed a confession that he had been reconciled and since then had not attended the Protestant services.

St. John Rigby was chained and remitted to Newgate. On three occasions, from his trial until his death, he was offered his liberty if he conformed. He was executed on June 21, 1600 at Southwark, at the very spot where two years before his reconciler, St. John Jones, O.F.M., had been done to death. The last words of St. John Rigby, the layman-martyr, were: "God forgive you. Jesus receive my soul."

25. St. Anne Line
Widow
Tyburn
February 27, 1601

St. Anne Line's father was so ardent a Calvinist that he disinherited Anne and her brother when they became Catholics. Anne married Roger Line, a convert like herself. Shortly after their marriage he was apprehended for attending Mass. After a brief confinement he was released and exiled to Flanders, where he died in 1594. Anne was widowed in her twenties. Though continually in ill health she gave her widowhood to caring for hunted priests. When Father Gerard, S.J., established in London a house of refuge for such priests, he placed Mrs. Line in charge. After Father Gerard's escape from the Tower in 1597, and with the authorities beginning to suspect her assistance, Anne Line moved to another house, which she made a rallying place for neighboring Catholics. The fatal raid was made on February 2, 1601, just a few minutes before Mass was to have begun. The priest managed to escape. But Anne's altar was there, with all its decorations — for it was Candlemas Day. The altar was the vital evidence. Mrs. Line was arrested and tried for harboring a priest. She was so sick that at her trial she had to be seated in a chair. In replying to the charge of harboring a priest, she spoke loudly so that all could hear her: "My lords, nothing grieves me more but that I could not receive a thousand more!" The valiant woman was sentenced to be hanged. On February 27 she was drawn to the gallows of Tyburn. Praying, kissing the timbers and proclaiming her Catholic Faith, St. Anne Line achieved the martyrdom for which she had prayed unremittingly.

Martyrs under King James I

In the year following King James' accession an *Act for the due execution of the Statutes against Jesuits, Seminary Priests and others* confirmed the existing penal laws. The Gunpowder Plot of 1605 led to still more persecutions. A new oath of allegiance, which was impossible for Catholics to take, was enforced by new acts, such as *For the better discovering and repression of Popish Recusants.* Most of the martyrs during the reign of James I were offered their freedom if they would take the oath.

26. St. Nicholas Owen, S.J.
Lay-Brother
Tower of London
March 12, 1606

St. Nicholas Owen, lay-brother of the Society of Jesus, devoted almost twenty years of his life to constructing secret places to hide priests from the pursuivants. Diminutive in size he was commonly and affectionately known as "Little John." He became a Jesuit before 1580. For eighteen years he rendered most dependable services to the English superiors, Father Henry Garnet and Father John Gerard. He was captured with Father Gerard, escaped from the Tower, and contrived Father Gerard's marvelous escape from that prison.

Little John's chief employment was in constructing "priest holes," as they were called. Tirelessly he dug underground passages, fashioned closets behind walls, erected false chimneys, or built recesses under floors or roofs. The work was all so laborious for this diminutive artisan. It was ever the loneliest of tasks, for secrecy precluded any assistants. It was the first part of Little John's martyrdom.

But Father Gerard understood the worth of these toilings; thus he wrote in his *A Narrative of the Gunpowder Plot:* "I verily think that no man can be said to have done more good, of all those that laboured in the English vineyard. For, first, he was the immediate occasion of saving the lives of many hundreds of persons, both ecclesiastical and secular, and of the estates also of these seculars, which had been lost and forfeited many times over if Priests had been taken in their houses; of which some have escaped, not once but many times, in several searches that have come to the same house, and sometimes four or six Priests together at the same time. Myself have been one of seven that have escaped the danger at one time in a secret place of his making. How many Priests then may we think this man did save by his endeavors in the space of seventeen years,

61

having laboured in all shires and in the chiefest Catholic houses of England?" These houses, it should be noted, were the sources for the keeping of the Catholic Faith not only by their residents but by the yeomanry round about.

St. Nicholas Owen's final arrest came in 1606. Waade, the keeper of the Tower, used the Topcliffe Rack during the terrible questionings. By this method of torture the arms were stretched above the head and joined together by an iron ring which was hooked to a rafter. The body was dangled considerably above the floor, and the heavy weights were attached to the feet. St. Nicholas' agony was painfully increased by his sufferings from a hernia. He was thus suspended on numerous days, sometimes for a period of six hours. During these agonies Waade questioned him interminably. Little John answered not a word, speaking only to God and invoking Jesus and Mary. His sufferings cannot be described, especially after the hernia broke. Then his end came. Dying for the primacy of the Holy Father

and for the Mass, St. Nicholas Owen, S.J.,
(or might one not say Saint "Little John"?)
entered into the white-robed army of the
martyrs.

27. St. Thomas Garnet, S.J.
Tyburn,
June 23, 1608

After severe disappointments trying to reach the continent for his priestly studies St. Thomas Garnet succeeded. He was ordained in 1599. He returned to England, where as he says: "I wandered from place to place, to reduce souls which went astray and were in error as to the knowledge of the true Catholic Church." During the excitement over the Gunpowder Plot he was arrested and severely handled in the Tower to force him to give evidence against his uncle, Father Henry Garnet, S.J., the unfortunate, though innocent, suspect in the plot. Though no connection could be proved, Father Thomas was kept in hard detention for seven months. Then together with forty-six other priests he was expelled to Flanders. Before the boat left, a royal proclamation was read to the priests threatening them with death if they returned. Father Thomas came back in 1607, only to be arrested within six months by an apostate priest. He was offered his life if he would take King James' oath. He steadfastly refused. He was then condemned for his Roman priesthood and for his return to England. St. Thomas Garnet, S.J., was hanged at Tyburn, June 23, 1608. Up to the last he was pressed to save his life by taking the oath. As though in reply, openly on the scaffold he declared himself a priest and a Jesuit. He died protesting that he was "the happiest man this day alive." His body was not cut down until he was dead.

28. St. John Roberts, O.S.B.
Tyburn
December 10, 1610

St. John Roberts was born in Wales, was converted in Paris through the influence of a fellow-countryman, and was the founder of St. Gregory's Monastery at Douay (now Downside in Somersetshire). He returned to England in April, 1603, coming in disguise, wearing a plumed hat, doublet and sword. His career was certainly a busy one: four times he was arrested, imprisoned and exiled; and four times he returned. In 1603 Dom Roberts most zealously served the plague-stricken people of London.

St. John made his last return in 1610. On December 2 the priest-hunters seized him just as he was concluding Mass; they took him to Newgate in his vestments. At the trial he refused King James' oath and revealed that he was both a priest and a monk. The Bishop of London, seated among the judges, railed against him as a seducer of the people. St. John answered: "Then were our ancestors deceived by blessed St. Augustine, the apostle of the English, who was sent here by the pope of Rome, St. Gregory the Great.... I was sent here by the same Apostolic See that sent him before me." St. John Roberts, O.S.B., was hanged at Tyburn on December 10, 1610.

29. St. John Almond
Seminary Priest
Tyburn
December 5, 1612

St. John Almond was a Lancashire man, born near Liverpool about 1577. He spent his boyhood and early manhood in Ireland. In his twentieth year he entered the English College at Rheims and later the English College at Rome. He finished his academic career so brilliantly as to gain the congratulations of Venerable Cardinal Baronius. St. John was always an exceptionally learned priest. His contemporaries considered him equally bold and zealous. In 1602 he was sent on the English mission. He labored for ten years in this apostolate. Once he was arrested in 1608, and again in 1612. The escape of seven priests from prison in that year sharpened the zeal of the persecutors. Dr. King, the Bishop of London, was especially irritated with St. John. The faithful priest refused King James' impossible oath of allegiance. After nine months in Newgate prison he was condemned as a Seminary priest. Standing by the gallows at Tyburn he answered the objections of a minister in the crowd; and he still displayed his great acuteness in argument. St. John Almond died on December 5, 1612, with the name of Jesus on his lips.

The Forty Martyrs

Martyrs under Charles I

The persecution was now an act of the Puritan majority of the nation forcing its will on an unwilling sovereign. On March 31, 1628, Parliament petitioned for more rigorous execution of the recusancy laws. It also passed an act "against sending any beyond the seas to be Popishly bred."

30. St. Edmund Arrowsmith, S.J.
Lancaster
August 23, 1628

St. Edmund was born in Lancashire of sturdy yeoman stock, tenaciously loyal to the old religion. His father and mother suffered much for their recusancy. Once their home was ransacked at night by pursuivants hunting for priests and they both were carried off to Lancaster jail. They were even forced to leave their four little children, including Edmund, in the lonely wrecked house, shivering in their night clothes.

The future martyr entered Douay in 1605, but owing to ill health he was not ordained until 1612. Lancaster was the scene of the sixteen years of his apostolate. And it was an intensive one; for he gloried in controversy and ignored all dangers. Such was his fervor and zeal that the prosecutor at his trial declared that left to himself alone he would have converted all of Lancashire. St. Edmund entered the

Jesuit Order in 1628, just previous to his apprehension. At the Lancaster Assizes for June, 1628, he was condemned for treason because he was a Jesuit priest and a converter of Englishmen to the Church of Rome. For two days before his execution, heavily manacled, confined in a cell where it was impossible to lie down and seemingly deprived of food, he was allowed to see no more, except a Protestant minister. St. Edmund Arrowsmith, S.J. was hanged at Lancaster on August 23, 1628. His last words were, "Bone Jesu."

31. St. Ambrose Barlow, O.S.B.
Lancaster
September 10, 1641

In 1614 a young man was accepted as a novice by the English Benedictines at Douay. His name was Barlow, he came from Lancashire, and he already had been imprisoned in London for the Catholic Faith. He was given Ambrose for his name in religion. Ordained in 1617 he was shortly after sent to his native country. There Father Ambrose labored for twenty-three years; and the Lancashire fold revered and loved him for his priestly zeal and his personal piety. In 1628 he administered the last sacraments to his friend, St. Edmund Arrowsmith, before the latter's martyrdom.

St. Ambrose's own sacrifice was to come thirteen years later. But during that period the gentle priest was four times arrested, and four times released. The Puritan-dominated Parliament now forced far sterner methods from Charles I. St. Ambrose was apprehended for the fifth and last time. On Easter Sunday, May 25, 1641, the Vicar of Eccles, clad in a surplice, led 400 men, armed with swords or clubs, to Morleys Hall (near Manchester) and seized Father Barlow as he was preaching at Mass. They carried him off to Lancaster. After four months in the castle he was brought to trial. St. Ambrose admitted his priesthood. When questioned about the penal laws, he boldly condemned them as unjust and barbarous. His liberty was promised to him if he would cease seducing the King's subjects. He answered courageously that he was not a seducer but rather a reducer (a leader of a return) bringing back the people to the true and ancient religion. He was adjudged guilty of treason on September 9, and on the following day he was executed. He walked slowly three times around the gallows, reciting the Miserere. St. Ambrose, faithful son of St. Benedict, was done to death with all the barbarities on September 10, 1641.

32. St. Alban Roe, O.S.B.
Tyburn
January 21, 1642

St. Alban Roe, a native of Suffolk and a Cambridge student, was converted by a conversation with a Catholic prisoner at St. Albans. He became a monk with the English Benedictines in Lorraine. After ordination in 1615 Father Alban was sent to England, where he remained for twenty-seven years, twenty-three of which he spent in various prisons. Yet in the few years of his freedom he proved a successful missioner. On January 19, 1642, he was tried for treason and condemned. His treason was his priesthood. Placed on the same sled to Tyburn with St. Alban was an eighty-year-old Seminary priest, Blessed Thomas Greene. This venerable missioner had served nearly fifty years in England, and for the last fourteen had been held in prison under death-sentence. The aged veteran was terrified at what he was soon to endure. But Father Alban Roe, ever a man of lively disposition, banished the old priest's fears. At the scaffold were three felons awaiting execution. The zealous Benedictine at once went to work to save the criminals' souls. When he turned from them to speak to the assembled crowd, he began cheerfully, "Here's a jolly company." St. Alban and Blessed Thomas were hanged simultaneously on the same gibbet. Their day of martyrdom was January 21, 1642.

33. St. Henry Morse, S.J.
Tyburn
February 1, 1645

St. Henry Morse led a full life in the service of the Church. He was born a Protestant, but became interested in Catholicism while studying law in London. He was received into the Church in Douay in 1614, was ordained in Rome and sent to England in 1624. Shortly after landing at Newcastle he was arrested and imprisoned at York Castle for three years. Just previous to his capture Father Morse had been ·admitted into the Society of Jesus; he made his novitiate under a fellow prisoner, Father John Robinson, S.J. On his release he served as a chaplain to the English regiments in Flanders.

Back in England in 1633 Father Morse labored in London for three years. He served heroically the victims of the plague of 1636. He visited 400 stricken families; and several of them were Protestants. He caught the plague, but recovered. The report of his having converted ninety

Protestant families brought about his arrest. Since he was only found guilty of being a priest, his sentence was deferred. He was freed on bail in 1637 and went into exile in Flanders. Again he acted as chaplain to English troops in the Spanish service. In 1643 Father Morse resumed his work in the North of England. After a year and a half he was apprehended and sent to London. In 1645 he was tried at the Old Bailey and was condemned on his previous commitment.

On the morning of his execution St. Henry arose at 4 a.m., offered a votive Mass of the Holy Trinity in Newgate jail, distributed Holy Communion, recited his Breviary, visited other condemned prisoners, and at 9 a.m. was laid on the sled and dragged to Tyburn. To the great crowd assembled at the gallows St. Henry declared that he was being put to death only for his religion. St. Henry Morse, S.J., had died as he had lived: to bring England back to the Catholic Faith and to her ancient acceptance of the Pope of Rome. His martyrdom occurred on February 1, 1645.

34. St. John Southworth
Seminary Priest
Tyburn
June 28, 1654

St. John Southworth was born of a Lancashire family, staunchly Catholic despite persecutions and impoverishments through all the penal times. He was ordained at Douay, and sent to Lancashire in 1619. After eight years of missionary work Father John was arrested and condemned as a priest, and as one functioning on English soil. While in prison he gave absolution from his cell window to St. Edmund Arrowsmith, who had made a sign to him for it as he was being led to execution. Father Southworth was transferred to the Clink prison in London. From then on his career is hard to follow; he was in and out of various London prisons; he was released more than once, and sometimes he was given leave to come and go. One thing does stand out, his heroic work for the victims of the plague of

79

1636. With St. Henry Morse he fearlessly visited the homes of the infected. When St. Henry was stricken St. John had to bear the heavy tasks all alone. As afflicted Catholic households were denied official relief, these two priests had to raise and distribute funds the best they could. They saved many bodies, and as priests they saved many souls. St. John's final arrest came in 1654. At his trial in the Old Bailey he insisted on pleading guilty to being a priest. He was condemned, and on June 28, 1654, he was executed. The body of the martyr was not mutilated; it was bought by the Spanish Ambassador and presented to Douay College. At the time of the French Revolution four students, to prevent profanation, secretly buried the body and its casket in the basement of the college. All memory of it was lost until 1927, when a French workman discovered the casket in the old foundations. The remains of St. John Southworth are now enshrined in Westminster Cathedral, in the Chapel of St. George and the English Martyrs.

The Forty Martyrs

Martyrs of the Popish Plot

The Popish Plot was one of the most infamous falsities in history. It was put forth as a plot organized by the Pope, the Jesuits and all other English priests, the Catholic Queen, the Catholic nobility and the Catholic rulers on the continent, to murder King Charles II and to wipe out English Protestantism. There was not one line of truth in it, for there was no such plot. The lying canard was concocted by high-placed politicians, and was spread over the whole nation by a collection of wretched perjurers. The leader of these last scoundrels was Titus Oates after whom the dastardly business is more commonly

81

known. The aims of the politicians and perjurers were: first, to exclude the Catholic Duke of York (James II) from the throne; and second, to banish Catholicism from the kingdom. A furious storm of fanaticism possessed the people and the courts. Before it subsided thirty-eight innocent men were judicially murdered. In the number of these unfortunate victims were the last six of the Forty Martyrs.

35. St. John Plessington
Seminary Priest
Chester
July 19, 1679

St. John was born in Lancashire and studied at the English College in Valladolid. Scarcely anything is known about his apostolate except that he served at Holywell (St. Winifred's Well) in Flintshire, North Wales. In his speech at the gallows he maintained that he was being done to death for his priesthood. He prayed for the King and the people of the realm. Finally he recommended himself to the mercy of Jesus, ending with the words, "O Jesus, be to me a Jesus." St. John Plessington was executed at Chester on July 19,1679.

36. St. Philip Evans, S.J.
37. St. John Lloyd
Seminary Priest
Both died at Cardiff
July 22, 1679

St. Philip Evans, a Welshman, was born in Monmouthshire, 1645, was educated at Saint-Omer, joined the Society of Jesus, 1665, and was ordained at Liége and sent to South Wales in 1678. He was unmolested until the Titus Oates Plot. Then a local official, an indefatigable priest-hunter, offered 200 pounds for his arrest. Father Evans, refusing to abandon his people, was captured in Glamorganshire, December 4, 1678, and imprisoned in a dungeon of Cardiff Castle. In a few weeks he was joined by St. John Lloyd, also a Welshman; he was a native of Brecknochshire. Father John was a Seminary priest. He had studied at Valladolid, where he took the oath to go on the English mission. He too, was captured in Glamorganshire.

84

After five months both priests were tried together. The chief witness against Father Philip was an apostate. Both were condemned, not for complicity in the fictitious plot, but for being priests who had come into the realm contrary to the laws of Elizabeth. Their treatment in prison allowed some liberties. Father Evans was actually engaged in a tennis game when it was announced to him that he was to die on the next day. So rejoiced was he at the news, that he insisted on finishing the game. The execution took place at Gallows Field in Cardiff. St. Philip Evans, after addressing the crowd in Welsh and English, died first. St. John Lloyd made but a few remarks, pleading humbly his lack of facility as a speaker. But he did say: "I die in the true Catholic and Apostolic Faith, according to these words in the Creed, *I believe in the Holy Catholic Church.*"

38. St. John Wall, O.F.M.
Worcester
August 22, 1679

Like so many missioners St. John Wall
had to use several aliases to shield him in
his apostolate. St. John used five. John
Wall was born of a strongly Catholic
family in Lancashire in 1620, the year of
Plymouth Rock. He studied at Douay and
at the English College of Rome. He was
ordained in 1645 and three years later was
sent to the English Mission. He became a
Franciscan in 1651 at St. Bonaventure
Friary in Douay. Friar John returned to
England in 1656 and labored in Worcester-
shire for twenty years.

He was discovered accidentally in
1678. On his refusing to take the Oath of
Supremacy he was committed to Worcester
Jail. At his trial he was charged with his
priesthood and of refusing the religious
oaths. One of the witnesses against him
was a man whose vices he had rebuked.
Sent to London St. John was interrogated
four times by Oates, Bedloe and other

promoters of the "plot." They failed to implicate him in any way in the fictitious conspiracy. His innocence was declared and, significantly, he was offered his life if he would abjure his religion. St. John was brought back to Worcester to be executed. On the previous day a fellow Franciscan obtained permission to visit him, and so was able to hear Friar John's confession and to give the last Holy Communion. At the actual execution the same Franciscan was able to give at the very final moment the last absolution to the martyr-friar. St. John Wall made the supreme sacrifice on August 22, 1679.

39. St. John Kemble
Seminary Priest
Hereford
August 22, 1679

St. John Kemble was the grand old man of the martyrs. He was eighty years old at his death, and he had been fifty-fours years engaged in priestly labors. He was born in Herefordshire in 1599. He studied at Douay, was ordained there in 1625, and four months later set out for England. His apostolate was in Herefordshire and in the adjoining parts of Wales. He seems to have been partly Welsh. His ministry was a hidden one. Little is known about him, save that the memory of his goodness lasted long in Monmouthshire, almost to the present day.

The fierce storm of the "Popish Plot" reached Hereford in the autumn of 1678. Father John, now a venerable old man, was arrested shortly and lodged in Hereford Jail. He was condemned in the following March for being a priest. Together with an old friend, Father David Lewis, S.J. (called also Charles Baker, S.J.), he was summoned to London. Both priests were to be interrogated by Oates and his evil confederates about complicity in the "Popish Plot." The journey, made in early spring, was very hard for both of the old priests. Because of physical disabilities it was excruciatingly painful for Father John. The interrogations were value-less, except that the innocence of both priests was clearly established. On Father Kemble's return he was kept in Hereford Jail for three more months.

The day of St. John Kemble's execution was August 22, 1679. When the under-sheriff came to the prison to lead him to the gallows, the old priest asked that he might be allowed to finish his prayers. It was granted. Then Father Kemble said that he would like to smoke one last pipe of tobacco and drink a last glass of wine. The under-sheriff agreed, and smoked a pipe himself to keep the old hero company. In fact he also furnished two cups of wine. This incident began the Herefordshire custom of calling the last pipe of a sitting "the Kemble pipe." The martyrs were holy, they were brave, and they were human.

40. St. David Lewis, S.J.
Usk
August 27, 1679

St. David Lewis, a native of Monmouthshire, was brought up a Protestant due perhaps to his father, a lax Catholic, for his mother was a very devout one. He was converted to Catholicism in his early manhood on a visit to France. He lived with his parents until their deaths; his father was reconciled to the old Faith. Young David strongly desired to be a priest. He studied at Rome and was ordained there in 1642. Two years later he joined the society of Jesus. In 1648 he returned permanently to the English mission, and was assigned to South Wales, where he labored zealously for twenty-eight years. To avoid the persecutors he used to make long and dangerous journeys at night that he might be able to visit the faithful under cover of darkness. He was known by the title "Father of the Poor."

In the "Popish Plot" frenzy St. David was arrested in Monmouthshire, and was imprisoned at Monmouth, and later at Usk. At his trial in Monmouth, March 28, 1679, as he could not be connected with the false "plot," he was condemned for being a priest in violation of the laws of Elizabeth. He was reprieved until he could testify to the questions of Oates, Bedloe and company. Father Lewis' journey with Father John Kemble has been told in the previous sketch. The real purpose of summoning Father Lewis to London was to have him save his life either by apostatizing or by inculpating others in the fictitious plot. No doubt the same was hoped of Father Kemble. The two old heroes stood their ground. St. David Lewis, S.J. was executed at Usk on August 27, 1679. Under the shadow of the scaffold he summarized his life: "My religion is the Roman Catholic; in it I have lived above these forty years. In it I now die, and so fixedly die, that if all the good things in this world were offered me to renounce it, all should not remove me one hair's breadth from my Roman Catholic Faith."

The Roman Pilgrims' Hymn

Full in the panting heart of Rome,
　　Beneath the apostle's crowning dome,
From pilgrims' lips that kiss the ground,
　　Breathes in all tongues one only sound:
"God bless our Pope, God bless our Pope,
God bless our Pope, the great, the good."

The golden roof, the marble walls,
　　The Vatican's majestic halls,
The note redouble, till it fills
　　With echoes sweet the seven hills:
"God bless our Pope, God bless our Pope,
God bless our Pope, the great, the good."

Then surging through each hallowed gate,
　　Where martyrs' glory in peace await,
It sweeps beyond the solemn plain,
　　Peals over Alps, across the main:
"God bless our Pope, God bless our Pope,
God bless our Pope, the great, the good."

From torrid south to frozen north,
　　That wave harmonious stretches forth,
Yet strikes no chord more true to Rome's
　　Than rings within our hearts and
　　　　homes:
"God bless our Pope, God bless our Pope,
God bless our Pope, the great, the good."
CARDINAL WISEMAN

DAUGHTERS OF ST. PAUL

Boston, Mass. 02130 - 50 St. Paul's Avenue
Boston, Mass. 02111 - 172 Tremont Street
Staten Island, N.Y. 10301 - 78 Fort Place
Bronx, N.Y. 10458 - 625 East 187th Street
Buffalo, N.Y. 14203 - 525 Main Street
Bridgeport, Conn. 06603 - 202 Fairfield Avenue
Cleveland, Ohio 44114 - 415 Euclid Avenue
Philadelphia, Pa. 19147 - 1127 South Broad Street
Miami, Florida 33137 - 2700 Biscayne Blvd.
Metairie, New Orleans, La. 70002 - 4403 Veterans Blvd.
Alexandria, La. 71301 - 86 Bolton Avenue
San Antonio, Texas 78205 - 114 East Main Plaza
San Diego, Calif. 92101 - 1570 Fifth Avenue
Oakland, Calif. 94612 - 278 - 17th Street
San Francisco, Calif. 94105 - 587 Market Street near 2nd St.
Toronto 10, Ontario, Canada - 1063, St. Clair Avenue West
London W. 8, England - 57, Kensington Church Street
Sydney 2140, Australia - 58, Abbotsford Rd., Homebush, N.S.W.
Pasay City - Manila, Philippine Islands - 2650, F.B. Harrison,
        P. O. Box 3576
Bombay, 50-AS, India - 143 Waterfield Rd., Bandra
Lagos, Nigeria - 35, Jones St., P. O. Box 3243